T5-AFH-911

101 Winning Monologues for Young Performers
Including Valuable Acting Hints

by Mark Weston

Single copies of plays are sold for reading purposes only. The copying or duplicating of a play, or any part of play, by hand or by any other process, is an infringement of the copyright. Such infringement will be vigorously prosecuted.

Baker's Plays
7611 Sunset Blvd.
Los Angeles, CA 90042
bakersplays.com

NOTICE

This book is offered for sale at the price quoted only on the understanding that, if any additional copies of the whole or any part are necessary for its production, such additional copies will be purchased. The attention of all purchasers is directed to the following: this work is fully protected under the copyright laws of the United States of America, the British Commonwealth, including Canada, and all other countries of the Copyright Union. Violations of the Copyright Law are punishable by fine or imprisonment, or both. The copying or duplication of this work or any part of this work, by hand or by any process, is an infringement of the copyright and will be vigorously prosecuted.

This play may not be produced by amateurs or professionals for public or private performance without first submitting application for performing rights. Licensing fees are due on all performances whether for charity or gain, or whether admission is charged or not. Since performance of this play without the payment of the licensing fee renders anybody participating liable to severe penalties imposed by the law, anybody acting in this play should be sure, before doing so, that the licensing fee has been paid. Professional rights, reading rights, radio broadcasting, television and all mechanical rights, etc. are strictly reserved. Application for performing rights should be made directly to BAKER'S PLAYS.

No one shall commit or authorize any act or omission by which the copyright of, or the right to copyright, this play may be impaired. No one shall make any changes in this play for the purpose of production.

Publication of this play does not imply availability for performance. Both amateurs and professionals considering a production are strongly advised in their own interest to apply to Baker's Plays for written permission before starting rehearsals, advertising, or booking a theatre.

Whenever the play is produced, the author's name must be carried in all publicity, advertising and programs. Also, the following notice must appear on all printed programs, "Produced by special arrangement with Baker's Plays."

Licensing fees for 101 WINNING MONOLOGUES FOR YOUNG PERFORMERS are based on a per performance rate and payable one week in advance of the production.

Please consult the Baker's Plays website at www.bakersplays.com or our current print catalogue for up to date licensing fee information.

Copyright © 2006 by Mark Weston
Made in U.S.A.
All rights reserved.

101 WINNING MONOLOGUES FOR YOUNG PERFORMERS
ISBN **978-0-87440-262-9**
#1543-B

ABOUT THE AUTHOR

Mark Weston has been writing for over 30 years. Among his many credits include numerous plays as among many others, the critically acclaimed, BECKWOURTH, (placed into the Schomburg Library archives, Oct. 2004), BECKWOURTH...THE LATER YEARS, BAGELS AND LUCK, (which has been placed into the Library of Congress in Braille and on Tape) THE NINTH OF APRIL, (performed at West Point on April 9, and in perpetuity) I'M WITH YOU! SHOEHORN, SPLIT INFINITIVE, DE WITT C!, HARRY AND EDDIE and the musical LOUISE, starring Paige O'Hara the voice of Belle in Disney's Beauty and the Beast.

Screenplays include BECKWOURTH, CARNIVAL MAGIC, released by General Cinema, PERSHING, A NEW TOMORROW, SLADE, CRISPUS ATTACKS, and the documentary INCA REMEMBERED, which was the recipient of over 30 international awards. Mark has written for daytime serials, and game shows, including The College Bowl and The Price is Right. His books include BASEBALL BLOOPERS for Prentice-Hall, and WINNING MONOLOGUES FROM THE BEGINNINGS WORKSHOP, published by Bakers Plays, in 1994 and still in print. His plays are also being published by the latter publishers. BECKWOURTH was published and released for production and readings in May, 2005.

His new monologue books, 101 WINNING MONOLOGUES FOR YOUNG PERFORMERS INCLUDING VALUABLE ACTING HINTS, and 80 EXCITING ORIGINAL MONOLOGUES FOR ADULT PERFORMERS INCLUDING VALUABLE ACTING HINTS, are now, and soon will be available. These are original and genuine monologues for study and audition purposes. No speeches or recitations but true monologues.

Mark is and has been teaching writing at the Screen Actor's Guild conservatory in New York. He is a member of the Dramatist's Guild. He also has taught Writing/acting at the Beginnings Workshop for many years.

Mark has been an actor for over 50 years, and was a member of Lee Strasberg's first classes, starting in 1954. Mark continued studying with Mr. Strasberg for 11 years. Many of these acting hints derived from notes taken from those sessions.

Mark has appeared on Broadway, Off-Broadway, in many touring companies, and on the big screen. In addition he has been seen on numerous soap operas including THE GUIDING LIGHT, THE SECRET STORM, THE EDGE OF NIGHT...and ANOTHER WORLD... to name a few.

He has also been teaching acting/writing to teens for the past fourteen years at the Beginnings Workshop and five years at The American Dance and Theater Studio in Queens, New York. Teaching acting/writing for the renowned dancer Tommy Rail, at his workshop in Galveston, Texas. Taught acting and directed the musical BEST FOOT FORWARD (revised the script with the permission of the brilliant librettist/composer Hugh Martin) at the Glen Cove Solomon Schecter middle school.

MONOLOGUES
for
GIRLS

LIFE CAN BE A DREAM
Girl: Ages 6 - 9

Modeling's a drag! Hey! I'm really only seven...and it's all I've ever done since I was four. What's wrong? How would you like changing clothes all day? Strangers pinning your dress up in front, and down in back all the time? The hot lights. Mother always telling me to say no...no, not only to drugs...but to Doritos...'n Twinkies...'n Big Macs? Yeah, that's what I've got to put up with. Well, I won't be a model forever...because when I grow up...I'm getting into something a lot easier...I'm going to be Janet Jackson!

Acting tip:

RELAXATION IS THE KEY.

NOTHING STAYS THE SAME!
Girl: Ages 8 – 14

My brother Larry came home from college yesterday. We were all glad to see him. Larry was taller than dad. He even grew a moustache. Mom cried because he looked so different. He was. How? I'll tell you how...he called me...kid. He used to call me...sis. I suppose he just forgot. *(Starts to cry.)* He's going to be a doctor...so he'll have to be away a lot longer. Maybe years! I'm happy for him...but what hurts is we won't be doing much together like we used to. It's like...I lost a brother.

Acting tip:

MAKE THE EFFORT!

THIS IS IT!
Girl: Ages 9 – 14

Today's the day! I know it's not going to be easy, but dad and mom said if we wait any longer...we'll never do it! What if it doesn't work out? Why shouldn't it? Everybody keeps saying we should all get together. I mean look at us...you're a boy...and we're friends...you love math And I hate it...but it doesn't matter...we still like each other. You like chocolate ice cream and I like vanilla...big deal! So why shouldn't your collie get along with my new poodle?

Acting tip:

SUB-TEXT IS ALSO KNOWN AS AN INNER MONOLOGUE.

GIVE ME STRENGTH!
Girl: Ages 11 – 16

The doctor told me I was bulimic. I never thought I was...till he told me. He said that if I kept gorging myself and throwing up...I could find myself in a hospital...or even worse. But if I quit, I'll be as big as a house. Then do you think Fred'll ask me out again? Sometimes I want to hide in my room and never come out! Why? Because I'm ugly! It's not funny...I really am! No matter what I do it's never enough. Mother always expects me to be perfect! Always telling me how I can always do better. No, she doesn't know what I do in the bathroom. But I suppose the doctor'll tell her. Then what do I do? If I give it up...I'll never feel like I'm worth anything! I don't want to die...but living isn't much fun either! Now don't start lecturing me, too...look I've got to go...no, I'm not going to McDonalds...or Burger King...or Wendys...I'm going to church.

Acting tip:

MIX YOUR ART WITH YOUR CRAFT. WHILE STUDYING ACTING...APPLY WHAT YOU'VE LEARNED AT THE SAME TIME BY PERFORMING ON A STAGE.

WHAT A WASTE!
Girl: Ages 12 – 16

When I grow up...I'll never go on a date! It's such a waste of time. What do I mean? Well, I'll tell you. Everytime my sister Ruth goes out...she has to take a bath...and do her nails...and hair...fuss with her make-up for hours...and pick out what she'll wear...and act cute...and keep smiling at him. I'd rather watch T. V. or play house...or read my books. I mean, dating couldn't be so much fun...because, whenever Ruth comes home...her hair's always messy...her clothes are wrinkled...and her make up's missing. What kind of fun is that?

Acting tip:

ACTING IS BELIEVING.

CONFUSED
Girl: Ages 12 – 16

I want to be Madonna! I mean…she's like cool. She's got it togeth-er…and always does her own thing. Madonna never loses any sleep worrying about what people say. Maybe when she was my age…she wanted to be someone else like…Ann Margaret…or Jean Harlow…or Marilyn Monroe! It's really sad. I mean why would she or anyone want to be someone else? Unless they were unhappy at home, too.

Acting tip:

FIRST THE ACTION THEN THE WORD.

THE BUSY SIGNAL
Girl: Ages 14 – 18

Eric dear, I know I should have phoned before I came over, but I couldn't because...our phone went dead tonight. The phone company won't fix it until tomorrow. So, I thought you might have been trying to contact me...about going out this weekend...and couldn't. I mean we didn't set the date...but I'm free...and since you couldn't get through to me...I decided to let you know. How about going bowling...or to the flicks...we can see Tom Hanks? They've got a special at Red Lobster...we can share lobster and shrimp. I bought a real short red leather skirt that'll flip you out and a matching see-through blouse. *(Seductively)* My folks've gone away for the weekend. We can have the house all to ourselves. Interested? What? You called? Busy? When? Then why didn't you tell me before I made such a fool of myself? Well, if that's the way you are...I'm going to be busy this weekend! What nerve! Goodbye! *(EXITS)*

Acting tip:

USE YOUR SENSES.

ACT YOUR AGE!
Girl: Ages 14 – 17

Doris, y' know I'm glad I'm still a teen-ager. You heard me right…and I'm not kidding. Making everyone think you're older than you are…doesn't mean you've got it all together. What brought this up? Well, take Angela for instance. Yeah, the 15 year old blonde who keeps acting like she's 21…and turns a lot of us off. Sure, she dates older boys…but what's so great about that? Wanna know something? I'd rather act my age instead of trying to impress people that I'm so much older and wiser than I am. What's wrong with acting my age? It's like building a building…it takes time. You've got to start from the bottom until you reach the top. Shortcuts don't work. I enjoy being 16…don't you? If others won't accept me for my age…then it really doesn't matter…because they only want me for what I'm not…instead of what I am. Hey, we'll be adults soon…so where's the rush? I don't envy Angela…I really feel sorry for her.

Acting tip:

DON'T ACT…LIVE TRUTHFULLY ON STAGE.

SCALING THE HEIGHTS
Girl: Ages 12 – 16

Guess what I found out this morning? Go ahead and guess! I'll give you a hint…when I found out I felt like I was floating on air! No, daddy wasn't promoted and we're not moving to a bigger house. It isn't even that our newsboy Freddie finally asked me for a date…but I think he will. Give up? Well, I'll give you a hint. Notice anything about me? *(Spins around.)* Well, you're certainly not observant. I got on the scale this morning…and I lost not one…not two…but three pounds. I feel great! *(Dances and sings, from West Side Story.)* I feel pretty…oh, so pretty!

Acting tip:

WORK FOR CONTINUITY BY STARTING THE SCENE BEFORE YOU ENTER ON STAGE. WHAT YOU WERE DOING JUST BEFORE THE SCENE STARTED.

DOLLARS TO DONUTS
Girl: Ages 10 – 14

I've heard that money's the root of all evil. Well, I agree! Sure, it must be great to be rich...have all the clothes you want...see all the movies you want to see...own all the Billy Joel, Dion, Reba McIntyre CD's in the world...but then what? No, I'm not crazy. Y'know what else I heard? It's not where you go or what you do... it's who you're with. I may not end up the richest woman in the in the world...but I'll be the happiest.

Acting tip:

MEMORIZE YOUR DIALOGUE SO YOU WON'T HAVE TO THINK ABOUT THE WORDS.

MAKING IT!
Girl: Ages 12 – 15

(Excited) Did you hear I got 100 on my geography test? I really did! It's the first time! I'm so excited! I mean I always thought geography was the pits...reading about places I'll never see...or want to...figuring what river emptied into what ocean...or how tall Mount Everest is. Who cared? I used to hate hearing Mrs. Ross tell us about how it felt floating down the Seine on her vacation...or looking at the pictures she took of the Dead Sea. Boring. But you know what turned it around for me? Guess who joined our class last month. Jeff Mussleman. *(Screams)* The track star! Whenever I saw him run...I used to evaporate. And there he was sitting next to me! Well, whenever we had an assignment...I'd imagine he was with me. I'd look at him, and feel his arms around me as we ballooned over the Pyrenees...or standing hand in hand as we watched the sun rise over the Sahara...and gazing into his eyes as we stood on a ship's deck in the moonlight over the Pacific Ocean. I've really learned to love geography. *(Screams)* But the big news is that I may get 1000 on another subject because Jeff's going to be in my sex education class too.

Acting tip:

SENSES ON A STAGE MUST BE FOOLED...OR THEY WILL NOT ALLOW YOU TO USE THEM. THEY MUST NOT BE FORCED.

HELLO TOMORROW!
Girl: Ages 12 – 16

I don't know what it is...but I feel different. I never felt like this before. Suddenly everything's upside down. I know I don't look different...but I am. No, it's nothing to worry about...but I know nothing's ever gonna be the same. Remember when Carl gave you your first kiss? Or how you felt when you wore your first bra...and when you became an aunt? Carol, I'm 13 years old today...I'm a teenager...I'll be going to high school soon. Then college...get married...have children. It's scary!

Acting tip:

IT'S NOT HOW MANY YEARS YOU'VE HAD ON STAGE THAT MAKES YOU AN ACTOR; IT'S WHAT YOU HAVE DONE IN LIFE AND HOW COURAGIOUS YOU ARE TO RELIVE THOSE MOMENTS.

HARRIED
Girl: Ages 13 – 17

Well, I survived! It was the worst job I've ever had. Believe me, I'd rather tame lions...or wrestle alligators...or work at McDonalds than ever again be a baby sitter. The Megans said their five year old Andrew was a perfect child. Well, they lied! You remember McCauley Culkin in Home Alone? Well, he was an angel compared to that brat! Do you see my favorite locket? Yeah, the one Dave gave me? You're right, it's gone. I was just about to grab it from sweet Andrew before he threw it into the garbage disposal. I heard it being crunched! The next thing I know, fire engines and police cars are all around the house...after dear Andrew snuck away and called 911. We spent the rest of the night playing hide and seek. No! I didn't want to find him...he was trying to find me! I've decided when I get married and have children...they'll never be named Andrew!

Acting tip:

YOU CAN ONLY CONCENTRATE ON ONE MAJOR THING AT A TIME.

COVERING UP!
Girl: Ages 14-18

Nancy, *(Shrugs)* summer's over! I think it's always too short. For the last few weeks, it felt like the fun was coming to an end. Y' know what I mean? No...you're wrong...! like school. Don't you? Of course, you do. I mean we both get good grades. So what's the problem? *(eyes her figure)* Soon, I'll be wearing winter clothes...you know...woolens... sweaters...coats. It's depressing. Alright, I'll tell you what's wrong. You were at the beach...remember the new bathing suit I wore? You'd think I was a movie star, the way it attracted all those guys. I even gave some my phone number. Still can't figure it out? C'mon get real...how do I expect them to be interested...when they can't see what caught their eyes in the first place? Summer's just too darned short!

Acting tip:

ACTING IS THE ABILITY TO GET UNDRESSED EMOTIONALLY ON A STAGE.

FINICKY FRED
Girl: Ages 15 – 19

Where's Fred? Who cares! As far as I'm concerned he's history. That's right, we've split! So? Sure, I know we've been dating for awhile, but nothing lasts forever...especially when it comes to him! I know he's good-looking, and generous, and popular...but who wants to be with a guy who's always bitching and controlling everything. On our first date he brought me a bouquet of long stemmed roses. But why did he have to spend so much time deciding which colored vase he thought they'd look best in? He's changed the way I walk...talk...even told me what friends I should have. Remember the mini-mini I bought? Fred said it wasn't appropriate for him. So I had to change into slacks. This went on for months...until I had enough. What did it? He took me to dinner for my birthday...and as usual started ordering for me...I told him not to bother...that since this was going to be our last supper...I'd better get used to making my own decisions. Yeah, he was surprised...but how much can a girl take? It's great to be me again. I hate control freaks...don't you?

Acting tip:

MAKE EVERYTHING REAL AND PERSONAL.

I'VE GOT A SECRET!
Girl: Ages 14 – 17

I've got a secret, Bob. I wish I could tell you…but then it wouln't be a secret. What would you do if you knew something about someone you really liked, and it wasn't what they'd want anyone to know? If you told, you'd lose a friend…or worse. So let's pretend I never brought it up. Now, I'd really like to tell you…but it's too personal. I know I can trust you, but I'm not sure what'd happen if I did. Maybe we ought to forget about it…I mean it's something I've been wanting to tell you…but couldn't…unless you really wanted to know. All right, if it'd never go any further and you'll never mention it again? O. K.? I found out you've been going to summer school everyday on your vacation. Hey, I'm not upset because you failed your courses. I think it's great that you have to make up classes…because I thought you were seeing someone

Acting tip:

NEVER PLAY FOR THE RESULT.

DREAMS COME TRUE
Girl: Ages 14 – 18

Gerard, did you ever have a dream that seemed so real it stayed with you even after you wake up? Well, it happened to me last night. What was it? Well you know it was only a dream, but I could swear it was real. You really want to know about it? Well, I dreamt that you broke our date last night, yeah, I know you did...only instead of the excuse you gave me about having to study...I dreamt you spent the night at the movies with Colleen Kelly. Yeah, I know it's silly...but you had your arm around her and you both kept kissing the whole time. What's wrong...it was only a dream. You even wore you're new silk jacket...the one I helped you pick out. Gerard, I don't know why you're getting so uptight...because I only dreamt I went to the same movie and sat five rows back. Gerard, come back...all I want to know is...did you like the movie?

Acting tip:

ACT WITHIN YOUR OWN PERSON. ONCE YOU LOSE YOUR-SELF ON STAGE IS THE START OF FALSE ACTING.

A FAMILY AFFAIR
Girl: Ages 12 – 16

Daddy, I love you. But sometimes I'm afraid. We all are. You tell mommy you can drink or leave it alone...but why do you have to drink at all? Aren't' we enough for you? Is it more important to you than us? I know you've tried to kick the habit...but you won't go for help. Don't look away, daddy. And take off those ugly dark glasses. They can't hide what's bothering you. Won't you tell me? Janet said she sees you going into the Lucky Charm...after work. Why can't you just come home? We used to spend so much time together...now you hardly talk...and when you do it's hard to understand what you're saying. Daddy, I was proud of you once...and I wish you had the same feeling about yourself the way you used to. Do you hear me, daddy? Mommy told me it's either us or the bottle. Please do something...soon...and make it the right decision.

Acting tip:

DON'T ANTICIPATE.

WINDY WENDY
Girl: Ages 14 – 17

Well, I just found out why Wendy Miller's so popular. I mean she always gets more dates than anyone at Jackson High. Even more than Terry Phillips…or Kelly McLoud or Barbara Lane. Hey, you've got to admit they're all candidates for Prom Queen. Sure, Wendy's got a great figure…and terrific legs…but she's not what I'd call a beauty. On a scale from 1–10…I'd rate her a five. So how does she rate with all the guys? Remember how windy it was yesterday? Well, I caught Wendy on Slocum and Main wearing a flared skirt. Whenever she saw a guy she was interested in…she'd let it blow. It really worked. Gotta go. Where? Are you kidding? I'm gonna buy me a flared skirt.

Acting tip:

DO NOT CRITISIZE YOURSELF WHILE PERFORMING.

MR. NOBODY
Girl: Ages 15 – 19

Lamont Marshall's a genius! Yeah, he's cute too! And ambitious, and like mother says…a girls got to be out of her mind to pass on a guy like Lamont. Sure, I know he likes me, but I'm not interested! Never will be. Why? Look at me…I'm black. Yeah, I know Lamont is, too…but he's prejudiced! He's a Republican. He's got pictures of Reagan, and both George Bushs all over his room. Rarely dates any girl who's not high yellow or snow white. What a drip! I just know that if you looked at his driver's license…under race it'll say…unaffiliated!

Acting tip:

CONCENTRATE.

SWITCHEROO
Girl: Ages 14 – 18

I hate basketball! Don't look at me that way…I really hate basketball! Especially at Jefferson High! Yeah, I know I'm on the cheerleading squad, but what good does it do me? Most girls'll give anything to date a letterman…and I don't blame them. But our starting five are a bunch of stiffs! Sure, they're all dreams, but they haven't won a game in two years! Instead of celebrating…do some smooching…get closer and all that…all they want to do is mope! So what is a girl supposed to do? *(Smiles seductively.)* I figured it out. No, I'm not transferring to another school. Don't need to. I'll just wave my pom-poms elsewhere. What am I talking about? Who won the championship last year? You got it. Our football team. They're always on a high. And what's best is that they're eleven to choose from this time. *(Does a cheer.)* Go team!

Acting tip:

IT'S NOT THE MAKE BUT THE DO!

SECOND THOUGHTS
Girl: Ages 14 – 19

Dad's moving back home this week. He and mom said they were going to have a trial reconciliation. What the hell does that mean? Does he leave again when he needs reassurance about his manhood? That's why he left in the first place. They talk about married men having seven year itches...but mom and dad've been together for twenty! Does that mean he still has two more chances to sow his wild oats? Sure, it's good to have him around again, but it's not like buying a dress. If it doesn't fit...you can return it. No one loses any sleep over it. But what if I get used to having them in the same house again...and they split? Haven't I cried enough? Kept praying for them to stay together? Been jealous of families that are still together? Well, this time I'm going to handle things differently...like when they took their vows, mom and dad promised to stay married for better or worse...well, I'll just hope for the better...and be ready for the worse.

Acting tip:

FIND THE DIFFERENCE BETWEEN YOU AND THE CHARAC-TER...AND PLAY THE DIFFERENCE.

TAKE THE MOMENT
Girl: Ages 14 – 17

My dad's 40 years old. I mean, he doesn't look 40. Does he? He always exercises...and beats everyone at tennis. He's still got all his own teeth...and jogs three miles a day...every day. But he's 40 years old. Soon he'll be 50...then 60...then as old as grandpa. Y'know sometimes I think everything'll stay the same...but I know it won't. He's the best dad in the world. Doris, I've gotta go...I need to hug him before it's too late!

Acting tip:

MAKE EVERYTHING REAL AND PERSONAL. MAKE THE STAGE AS RECONIZABLE TO YOU AS IF YOU WERE IN YOUR OWN HOME OR IN ANY PLACE YOU KNOW.

TURNAROUND
Girl: Ages 15 – 19

I'm really fed up! No! I'm furious! It's the worst thing that could have ever happened! You know how long I was looking forward to the senior spring dance. I bought a special mini-skirt...and wild see-through blouse...and my first high-heeled pumps. So what happens? Mom says I've got to stay in bed because I caught the flu! It's not fair! Now Charlie's going without me. I'm sure he'll never forgive me for standing him up. Sure, he knows I'm sick...but he'll still be alone. I hope. *(Thinks)* I mean how long will the cats keep their claws off our star quarterback? He's only human...so I'm sure he'll be on the dance floor all night. Getting a lot of numbers. He won't have time to see me anymore. I get sick and he flies the coop. Y'know, I'm glad I'm sick...because now I know what kind of creep Charlie really is!

Acting tip:

LESS IS MORE!

CAST OFF
Girl: Ages 15 – 19

What do you do when you're at a dance…and the wrong guys ask you to dance with them? I mean you don't want to be rude or hurt their feelings. I know I wouldn't like to be turned down. But there's nothing worse than being close to someone you'd rather not be with. Well, you know what I do? Now keep it to yourself because they'll drown me if they found out. I just point at a girl on the dance floor and say, you see that pretty girl over there? She's been eyeing you…and since she's my friend…I wouldn't want her to get jealous. What if she doesn't like him? Then let her figure out her own excuse.

Acting tip:

AN OBJECT ALLOWS YOU TO DO WHAT YOU COULDN'T ORDINARILY DO.

COMPETITION
Girl: Ages 16 – 19

Keith Brant's a lost cause. Sure, I still like him…I guess. What's there not to like? He's smart…got it all over the other guys…never rushed me…never late…so everything was super…till he decided to be a jock! So, why is that such a problem? Well, it wouldn't be if he didn't spend so much time running marathons, lifting weights…and admiring himself in every mirror available. I mean what chance do I have? For the first time I've got competition! No, not his ex-girlfriend…no, he's not answering personals in newspapers or on the internet…or going to dances. So who's my competition? HIM!

Acting tip:

RELEARN YOUR SENSES: THROUGH SENSE MEMORY EXER-CISES.

WRONG NUMBER
Girl: Ages 16 – 19

I once was called easy. But that's before I knew better. The kids in school always teased me. Put me down. It didn't bother me because I had my own problems that were more important. What problems? Self confidence for one. Self esteem, too. I needed the attention I never got at home. So when I dressed sexy...or talked dirty...or flirted...I felt like I was someone. My father always made me call him by his first name, never dad or pop. Bob! Like he was just another guy, and I was just another girl. We were never close. Mom? She couldn't care less about me. I was just there. But now I've got my act together. What turned it around? Well, I watched the Oprah Winfrey show and heard something that made sense. A girl my age, and with my problems, said she straightened out when she decided that guys better take her for what she was...not...and for what she thinks she was! She wanted respect! It made sense. Now when a guy hits on me for my number I tell him it's 1-800-GET LOST!

Acting tip:

WHATEVER YOU ARE...USE IT!

TURNED ON!
Girl: Ages 16 – 19

Have you ever wondered what attraction is? Why does one guy make you feel like he's all you're been looking for...and others who are just as cool...mean nothing? You pass two great looking guys walking by, and you catch their eyes...and one turns you on. You don't speak to him...but for that moment...you're in love. The look in his eyes...his grin...maybe it's his cologne. I asked grandma...and you know what she told me? It's association. That sometime in the past...so long ago...you've forgotten...someone with a certain look...or smile...or even a laugh...did something that made you feel good. When it happens again...it turns you on. So, what's attraction? It's simple. It's association.

Acting tip:

THE DEFINITION OF THE 'METHOD' IS SIMPLY THE LABELING OF YOUR OBJECTS.

POOPED!
Girl: Ages 16 – 19

Guy is the laziest guy I ever met. He's always tired. If he tells me he's pooped again…I swear I'll scream! If he won the lottery, he wouldn't have enough energy to make a sound louder then… *(Softly)* wow. If Madonna visited him at his place; he'd yawn and tell her to leave her number…and he'd get back to her later. Much later! I saw him last night, and his mother made him his favorite night, and meal…pork chops and French fries…but he could hardly lift his fork…let alone clean the plate. What's wrong with him? Nothing, except for all those sexy exercise tapes he buys. You know…Jane Fonda's…Mary Tyler Moore's…Dolly Parton's. No, he doesn't' exercise…he gets his kicks just watching, them for hours. He gets so drained he can hardly lift himself off the couch. Well, I've decided that if we ever get married, and if It's going to last…we're definitely never going to own a VCR…or a DVD player!

Acting tip:

AN OBJECT IN ACTING IS LIKE A STRING TO PEARLS. THE OBJECT KEEPS THE WORDS TOGETHER LIKE THE STRING HOLDS THE PEARLS.

HELLO AGAIN!
Girl: Ages 17 – 19

(Looking into mirror.) Hi, I'm back. So what do you want me to say? He was everything he said he was over the phone? He wasn't. Like the rest of them. All he did was talk about himself. About the girl he broke up with…and that he was going to be an accountant…and about the car he was planning to buy…I mean we must have spent two hours at the diner and I don't think he learned a thing about me. Remember the guy who kept eyeing all the other girls? What about the one who kept picking at his teeth without covering his mouth. *(Imitating his gross vocal sound.)* "What's wrong? You were just singing and you didn't cover your mouth!" It's really frightening to think we may have to spend the rest of our lives looking…and having to deal with these no class degenerates. *(Eyes herself.)* You look pretty tonight. I love you hair. What a cute figure. And what's best is that I like you. Y'know the more blind dates I go on the more I know how much we've got on the ball. Someday, someone'll see us and they'll be all that we deserve. We'll both stand in front of this mirror and see two perfect matches, someday.

Acting tip:

AN ACTOR AND WRITER ARE LIKE FROZEN ORANGE JUICE…THE LATTER SUPPLIES THE JUICE AND THE FORMER SUPPLIES THE WATER.

BROTHERLY LOVE
Girl: Ages — Late Teens

Guess who I'm dating. No, not Cal…or Bill…or Frank. Give up? It's Skee! What's the look for? He's a great guy, and handsome, too! So what's wrong? Oh, I know. You don't think I should be dating my brother. Well, he's not my brother. Sure we live under the same roof, but I'm mom's daughter and he's dad's son! When they got married I wasn't too excited, but things have changed. Actually they're great! It's fun knowing Skee's getting ready in the next room…there's no reason to phone each other about being late…or even early. Not having mom or dad approve of my date. And if things work out like I think they will…we'll not only be husband and wife…but we'll also be step brother and step sister. Isn't that cool?

Acting tip:

DURING A COLD READING AUDITION…IF YOU DON'T UNDERSTAND WHAT YOU'RE READING ACCEPT THAT AS A FACT AND READ IN NEUTRAL, BUT ALLOW YOUR ANTEN- NAE TO FIND ASSOCIATIONS THEN SEE WHERE THEY TAKE YOU. IF DOESN'T WORK THEN GO BACK TO NEUTRAL AND WAIT FOR ANOTHER ASSOCIATION FROM YOUR LIFE.

FAILING GRADES
Girl: Ages 17 – 19

Larry, I don't think we should see each other anymore. Please, let me explain. It's important. I know we've been together for months but there's no future. Sure, we've had great times together...and I didn't expect it to end...but it's for the best. No, I'm not seeing anyone else...and you didn't do anything wrong. What happened? I was at the dentist yesterday...and picked up an old Cosmopolitan magazine in the waiting room. It had a compatibility test which I filled out. We failed! I know you never saw it, and since you weren't there...I answered for the both of us.

Acting tip:

REALLY LISTEN AND RESPOND.

FOREVER YOUNG
Girl: Ages 16 – 19

I visited grandma and grandpa last week…in Duluth. It was the first time since I was a baby. I mean it's so far away from Richmond. They showed me their wedding pictures. Grandma was gorgeous. I never knew she once was so beautiful. Her hair was dark, and long, and what a figure she had. I could swear she could have been a movie star. Sure, she's still pretty…but now her hair is grey, and she wears glasses…and has to use a cane, like grandpa. He was handsome, too, when they were young. What got me was the way they stared at each other…like they must have when they first met. Oh, grandma kept a neat house…but I suppose they didn't look at the album too often. When I grow old…I hope my husband and I don't need wedding pictures to remind us why we chose each other.

Acting tip:

ACTING IS LIKE A MUSCLE…IF YOU DON'T WANT TO LOSE IT…USE IT.

THE BIG SHOT
Girl: Ages 15 – 18

You're a braggart, Fred. Yes, you are. You make sure everyone knows you're the best…whether you are or not! Now don't interrupt…because it's time we had this out. You don't own a Cadillac…it's your fathers! You've told everyone that you're going to Harvard…State University isn't Harvard! The bullshit you've spread around about how you've inherited an endowment from your aunt…then why are you working part time in a shoe store? Look, it that's your thing…it's your business but why do you keep denying we're dating? Cheryl told me! Why shouldn't I believe her? She never lied to me before. Well, you don't have to worry about it…because for the first time you really told the truth! So long, Fred.

Acting tip:

EVERY PERFORMANCE NO MATTER HOW MANY TIMES YOU'VE DONE IT…SHOULD ALWAYS BE FOR THE FIRST TIME!

TATTLE-TALE
Girl: Ages 15 – 19

I guess you want to know about my date with Michael? About how he picked me up in his new Accura...and about the dozen long-stemmed roses he brought me...and how my parents like him...and the way he danced and held me all night at the Prom...and how all the girls were jealous of me...and how he kissed me goodnight...and said I was beautiful? I know how much you want to hear about it all...but y'know, I don't really feel like going into it, if you don't mind.

Acting tip:

THE ACTOR WHO RELIES ON NATURE'S ENDOWMENTS AND ON HIS OWN INDIVIDUALITY IS THE CREATIVE ARTIST.

SAFETY LAST
Girl: Ages 16 – 19

Why is it that whenever I have a date…my parents put him through the third degree…like he was a criminal. How old are you? What kind of grades do you have? What's your religion? Are you on drugs? Are you a reckless driver? What are your intentions? The guys are really turned off and I never hear from them again. I know dad and mom are concerned about my safety…and future…but if this keeps up…I may become the safest old maid in history!

Acting tip:

PHYSICAL TENSION CANNOT BE RELIEVED UNLESS YOU ARE MENTALLY AWARE THAT IT EXISTS AND CAN PINPOINT ITS LOCATION.

NEIGHBORS
Girl: Ages 16 – 19

You won't believe this, but I met the man of my dreams at a dance last night. When our eyes first met…it was love at first sight. His name is Hal…and he looks like Tom Cruise…only handsomer. He even wore my favorite cologne…Obsession. *(Screams)* He's a great dancer…and is going to be a doctor. He even asked me out for New Years Eve…I know it's only August…isn't that great? They say love will find you when you least expect it…but it should have happened sooner…after all…we only live five blocks away from each other.

Acting tip:

WHEN PERFORMING A MONOLOGUE…TRULY LOOK AT THE PERSON YOU'RE IMAGINING IS ACTUALLY THERE. HIS OR HER HAIR…NOSE…EYES…CHIN…BODY. IT'S NOT THAT YOU SEE THE PERSON…BUT THAT YOU ARE TRYING TO SEE THEM.

TIME FLIES!
Girl: Ages 16 – 19

(Hysterical in her slip.) Oh, my God! It's almost seven! Gerald'll be here in fifteen minutes. Where the hell did the time fly? That's the last time I take a bath...before a date! What is wrong with me? I've waited so long for him to ask me out...and now I've got ten minutes to get ready! Sally...someday when you grow up...don't do what I just did! Look At my hair...it'll take me an hour to fix it...what am I going to do? What dress should I wear? Which shoes? We're going to dinner at a posh Italian restaurant and I'll have to look like a loser! He'll never ask me out again! Look at my face...I won't have time to put on my make-up. *(Puts on skirt.)* Oh, no...it's got a stain! What? No...sweetheart, I can't play house with you...maybe some other time...sister is going crazy! Where's my rouge? Where are my new patent leathers? *(Screams)* I'll never make it! *(Calls)* Mother! *(Listens)* I'll never be ready! Tell Gerald I'm sick! He's going to pick me up at seven! He should be here any minute! I just want to die! What? It's what? Only six? What are you talking about? Didn't I turn my clock back last night? Oh, no! Well, thanks...isn't that wonderful? I love daylight saving time!

Acting tip:

THERE'S NO REASON AN ACTOR COULD ALSO BE A WRITER...SINCE THEY BOTH USE THE SAME INSTRU-MENT...THEMSELVES!

THE SHOWDOWN
Girl: Ages 17 – 20

Tonight's the night! I was hoping it'd never come...but I knew it had to happen. Garry's been pushing for it for weeks...but I just wasn't ready. I'm still not. I know everyone does it in time...especially when they've been together for so long. And now it's finally going to happen. I kept giving Garry excuses...but they don't work anymore. He's been patient...but now he means business. What bothers me most is what happens if it doesn't work out? What if he's disappointed...then I may never see him again. I just don't what to do...but to got through with it. Remember Frank? Bruce? Hal? When it was over I never heard from them again. God, please let my parents finally approve of one of my boyfriends.

Acting tip:

ACTIONS SPEAK LOUDER THAN WORDS.

CAREERS
Girl: Ages 14 – 18

No matter how I feel, everyone thinks they know what's best for me...and they never stop telling me. You'd think I didn't have a mind of my own. Well, I'm freaked...and I'm not going to take it anymore. Would you believe grandma says I should be a doctor...like grandpa. Grandpa thinks I should be a librarian like grandma. Mom? She wants me to be a teacher. Dad's a lawyer so he wants me to be a legal secretary or paralegal. What's worse is that they never let up. What do I want? Well, I'm glad someone asked...it's simple...I just want to be left alone!

Acting tip:

ACTING CAN BE TAUGHT...BUT DRAMATIC ENERGY CAN NOT.

TIRED!
Girl: Ages 14 – 18

Janet…I don't feel like playing tennis today. I'm sorry. Maybe you ought to ask Helen…or Linda. I'm just too tired. I didn't get to sleep till three this morning. No, I felt all right….I just couldn't fall asleep. I don't know what it is. Maybe it was watching Friday the 13th on the late late show. Every time I see Freddie…he gets scarier and scarier. Maybe I ate too much at dinner…too late. All I want to do is collapse. I'm so bored. I feel like I'm thirty years old. No, I don't have to see a doctor…I just want to sleep and sleep and sleep. I may not get up for a week. I'm pooped! *(Listens)* Yes, mother? Who? *(Excited)* You're sure? *(Shrieks)* Wow! Janet…did you hear? Jimmy Blair's on the phone. Our quarterback! He's calling me! Janet, you've gotta excuse me. I've gotta go before he hangs up. He's calling me! *(Shrieks)* Can you believe it? Isn't it great? How's my hair? Do I need lipstick? What am I saying? Who's tired? I'll be back. Wait. *(Shrieks)* Mother! I'm coming! *(EXITS like an Olympic track star.)*

Acting tip:

AN AUDIENCE WANTS TO BELIEVE AND WILL IF YOU ARE BELIEVABLE.

MIXED FEELINGS!
Girl: Ages 17 – 19

Julie, when I got the letter that said I was accepted, I was delirious! It hit me that I was going to be a Princeton freshman! My first choice! It was a dream come true! I packed, and unpacked my bags for weeks! Kept reading about the school! Kept thinking of becoming a cheerleader! *(Does a cheerleader kick and waves an imaginary pom-pom.)* Well, I worked hard at high school...and it paid off! But when I thought about leaving home, *(Looks around her room.)* I had mixed feelings. It was like all that meant so much to me was coming to an end. The trees in the yard, my desk, with all the drawers filled with things I could never throw away. The pictures and memories on the walls. But when Spookie came in to say goodbye...I cried. He looked up at me with his spaniel eyes as if he was saying, 'Please don't leave.' Spookie's an old dog...and I knew that our days together may be over. Sure, I'm excited about graduating...and leaving for Princeton...but sometimes it's hard to say goodbye to what I once knew...and meant so much to me.

Acting tip:

FILLING YOUR RESUME WITH UNIMPORTANT CREDITS LIKE BATON TWIRLING, COOKING, BIKE RIDING ETC. ONLY SAYS HOW LITTLE EXPERIENCE YOU HAVE HAD.

FOREVER YOUNG!
Girl: Ages 17 – 20

I visited grandma and grandpa last week…in Duluth. I haven't seen them in years because they live so far. I wish you could meet them. They showed me their wedding pictures. Grandma was gorgeous. I never knew she was so beautiful. Her hair was dark, and long, and what a figure she had. I cold swear she could have been a movie star. Sure, she's still pretty...but now her hair is white, and she wears glasses…and has to use a cane like grandpa. He was handsome, too, and they both were so young…once. What got me was the way they looked at each other…like they must have when they first met. Their wedding album was dusty. When I grow old… I hope my husband and I won't need wedding pictures to remember why we chose each other.

Acting tip:

WHEN WORKING FOR PAIN IN A SCENE IT IS IMPORTANT IT DOES NOT HAVE ANY PSYCHOLOGICAL OR EMOTIONAL CON-NECTION TO YOUR PRESENT LIFE.

TAKING STOCK!
Girl: Ages 13 – 16

Cheryl, what do you think of Ellen? I mean how do you feel about her? You do? Well, I don't! She thinks she knows it all! Always bragging about the places her parents took her...her new clothes...making sure you know about the expensive labels...even how popular she is with all the lettermen! I really don't believe you can't see through her. Well, let me tell you...I do! From the time we met, I knew Ellen was a phony! She's not? Are you serious? Well, if you think so much of her...maybe I made a mistake about you! What? Who's jealous? I am not insecure! That's stupid! I know who and what I am...do you...jerk? What are you walking away for? Can't stand the truth? Boy, was I wrong about you! You and Ellen deserve each other! *(Starts walking away, stops, looks over her shoulder.)* What does she know? What do they all know? Jealous? That's a laugh! Insecure? Never! *(Upset, contemplating.)* Or am I?

Acting tip:

TRYING TO FIND AN AGENT BEFORE YOU LEARN YOUR CRAFT...IS LIKE PUTTING THE CART BEFORE THE HORSE.

TELEPHONITIS!
Girl: Ages 14 – 17

(Shrieks) I can't stand it! How much longer? I've never gone so long without it! When will it be over? I should've known this would happen when I needed it most! It's like I'm in a vacuum…worse…it's like I don't exist! It may be easy for you because you don't care…but I've got to have it! I'm not apologizing and you can't put me down for it. It's been over four hours now…I know it won't last forever…but I need it now! What is wrong with them? Don't they realize how much it means to be able to talk and hear from my friends? Damn the telephone company…they're ruining my social life… *(Listens)* Did you hear that? IT'S RINGING!

Acting tip:

FOLLOW YOUR DREAM AND YOU WILL NEVER HAVE TO REGRET NOT TRYING TO FULFILL IT.

SLOW POKE!
Girl: Ages 13 – 16

Hi, Jacky…no, don't wait up for me…I decided not to rush this morning Sure, I'm feeling just fine…I just don't feel like rushing. Yeah, I know I'll be late for school…so who cares? Look, don't let me keep you…I'll be leaving when I'm good and ready! Hey, get a life, will y'? I told you I feel fine…I'll get there when I get there. There you go again…hey, it's got nothing to do with you! It's nothing personal! All right…if you have to know, but I wish you'd keep it to yourself. It's Jerry Albright! He's become a school late monitor. I've been trying to find an excuse to talk to him for months…so I figure if I'm late…he'll have to get my name…room number…excuse…and maybe even my phone number. You never know what can happen next. *(Laughs)* I'm not as dumb as I look!

Acting tip:

I HAVE NEVER SEEN A CAST LEAVING A STAGE DOOR LOOK-ING DEPRESSED OR FRUSTRATED.

CONCERNED
Girl: Ages 13 – 17

Dad, did you ever know something about someone…but because you liked them, and didn't want to hurt their feelings, you kept it to yourself? But what if you thought they should know, I mean what if it was really important? Oh! But if you did tell it might ruin a friendship or even a family? I thought so, and I guess you're right. What are you worrying about? I just wanted your advice. No, it's got nothing to do with you…or mom…or any of the family. No, I didn't catch Harold smoking in the bathroom…no, mom isn't unhappy about your staying late at the office. At least, I don't think so. Of course she's not seeing anyone. Dad! I told you it's nothing to worry about. I just wanted your opinion. Now I found out what to do. Thanks.

Acting tip:

CASTING DIRECTORS USUALLY MAKE UP THEIR MINDS ABOUT AN ACTOR'S AUDITION WITHIN FIFTEEN SECONDS.

MONOLOGUES
for
BOYS

SAMSON
Boy: Ages 6 – 8

Hi, David. It's me, Sam! Didn't you recognize me? Maybe it's because I got my first haircut. Yeah, it finally happened. Isn't it great? Mom cried at the barber shop because she liked my long curls. She kept saying she was losing her little boy. Daddy always wanted me to get a haircut but mommy didn't. They had so many arguments about it. So, what changed Mom's mind? Daddy said, that since I was going to keep looking like a girl…he was going to buy me a dress!

Acting tip:

TRY TO RECAPTURE YOUR CHILDLIKE IMAGINATION AND BELIEVABILITY.

COMPROMISED!
Boy: Ages 6 – 9

Did you ever go to a lady doctor? I did today. Mom took me to the doctor's office because I had a stomach ache. I always went to Doctor Levy, but he's getting old, so he has a new partner, Dr. Garland. She asked me to come into her room and told me to get undressed. Mom stayed outside. It was worse than taking medicine. I jus stood there until Dr. Garland asked, "What's wrong?" I said, "You're a girl!" Yeah, I know she's a doctor, too…but I'm a boy. She should take care of girls. She said she couldn't examine me until I got undressed. Yeah…I did…after she promised to shut one eye!

Acting tip:

TRY TO REGAIN THE IMAGINATION OF YOUR CHILDHOOD. WHEN A CHILD PLAYS WITH DOLLS OR TRAINS ALL THEIR ACTIONS ARE DONE FULLY...BUT THIS ABILITY DECREASES AS THE CHILD AGES. INHIBITIONS MUST BE AVOIDED ON A STAGE.

STAR STRUCK
Boy: Ages 6 – 9

I'm gonna marry Shirley Temple. I see her all the time on television and on my video tapes. I like how she sings…and dances…and how pretty she is. I'm going to find out where she lives…on the internet, and send her my picture…then she'll send me hers…and we'll become friends…and when we grow up…we'll get married. What do you mean she's too old for me? I'm going to be seven!

Acting tip:

IF YOU CAN'T BE HEARD IN A THEATER…MENTALLY SAY TO YOURSELF THERE IS NO ROOF OVER THE STAGE.

SMALL TALK
Boy: Ages 6 – 10

(Sadly) I went to the doctor this morning because mom wanted me to have a check-up. He took my temperature…and put that thing on my chest…looked into my eyes…and ears…and even stuck a stick in my mouth and told me to say "aah." Yeah, he said I was fine. But I'm not. Why? He measured my height and I only grew three inches in six months! Three inches! Only three inches! What do you mean what's wrong with that? Everything! I really like Marilyn, and I'm still shorter than her. I'll never catch up.

Acting tip:

BE PROFESSIONAL. NEVER BE LATE FOR REHEARSALS …LEARN YOUR LINES…LISTEN TO YOUR DIRECTOR AND REMEMBER WHAT HE OR SHE ASKS YOU TO DO…KEEP YOUR PERSONAL PROBLEMS AWAY FROM CONCENTRATING ON YOUR ACTING TASKS. BE SERIOUS ABOUT BECOMING AN ACTOR.

MONEY TALKS
Boy: Ages 6 – 10

Donna's moving. Mom said the Graham's are going to Virginia. I don't know where…but I know it's far away. I like Donna. We always held hands in the halls. I gave her bubble gum…and Oreos…and sometimes I bought her an ice cream cone. I didn't care that I spent my allowance on her…and now she's going away. I'll never see her again. What did she give me? What do you mean? She gave me…she bought me…uh…nothing. Once I asked if I could take a sip out of her Coke…and she said…no! She told me to buy my own. Y' know…I don't care she's moving…Donna's selfish…and…she costs too much!

Acting tip:

CHOOSE EMOTIONAL OBJECTS THAT ARE AT LEAST FOUR OR MORE YEARS IN THE PAST. OBJECTS THAT ARE STILL TO BE RESOLVED CAN AFFECT YOUR PERFORMANCE. IF AN OBJECT IS THAT FAR IN THE PAST AND YOU STILL CAN RECALL IT…IT MUST HAVE BEEN QUITE MEMORABLE.

PROPHECY
Boy: Ages 7 – 10

Me and Gloria are going to go steady. I never thought it'd happen. I mean she's stuck up…and always keeps away from me. When I try to talk to her…she calls me shorty and says that she's busy. But I like her and think she's the prettiest girl in the whole school. What are you laughing for? Things are going to change…you'll see. Y' wanna know how I found out? It's simple. Yesterday, I was lying down on the school lawn and found a forget-me-not…plucked away…and that's when I found out…she loves me!

Acting tip:

TO KEEP YOUR MIND FROM CONCENTRATING ON THE AUDIENCE…MENTALLY CREATE A FOURTH WALL.

NO SALE!
Boy: Ages 7 – 12

(*Depressed*) Hi, Ken...what's wrong? Nothing. Naw, I'm not unhappy. I don't care what I look like...I'm fine! Will you quit? There's nothing wrong! Quit bugging me! I told you nothing's wrong! C'mon...aw shucks...all right, you really wanna know? It's Linda! Naw, we didn't have a fight. It was worse! This morning we decided to sell the apples from our trees. So we put stands in front of our houses...with signs...'Apples...ten cents apiece!' Y' they sold. So what's the problem? You know how cute Linda is...when she flutters her baby blues and talks so sweet...well, she sold all of hers and I've still got all of mine!

Acting tip:

SAY A LINE SMELLING AN IMAGINARY OFFENSIVE ODOR. USING THE SAME LINE SNIFF A SWEET IMAGNARY OBJECT. SENSES CAN BE MADE TO REACT AS THOUGH IT WERE THE REAL OBJECT.

BETTER LATE THAN NEVER!
Boy: Ages 7 – 12

Grandpa Frank took me to the ice ring again. He's nothing like other grandpas. When I go swimming...so does grandpa, Frank. If he sees me with a bat and ball...he wants to play, too. It's all right with me...but when we go ice skating it's a drag. He does a figure eight better than anyone. Especially me. I try but I can't get it right. Sure, grandpa tells me to keep practicing and tries to teach me...it's easy for him...he's been doing it a whole lot longer. No, he never shows off...he just knows how. Oh, I'm sure I'll get it...when I'm grandpa's age.

Acting tip:

THEATER IS LIKE A JEALOUS WOMAN. WHAT YOU GIVE IT...IS HOW MUCH YOU WILL RECEIVE IN RETURN.

LOOKING FOR LOVE!
Boy: Ages 7 – 11

(Carrying books.) Wow, are these books heavy! Yeah, I just got back from the library. I brought back the others and took these. They've got so many. Big ones...and small ones...in all colors. Yeah, I know I'm always carrying books. Why? Well, if I didn't...would we be talking now? A lot of people ask me why I'm carrying so many books...like you just did. Then they see what I'm reading...and they think I'm really smart. I guess I'll keep carrying books...till people pay attention to me without them.

Acting tip:

IN TRYING TO CREATE AN EMOTION FROM THE PAST...DON'T TRY TO REMEMBER HOW YOU FELT...BUT RECALL THE PHYSICAL EVENTS THAT YOU EXPERIENCED. WHAT YOU WERE WEARING..ODORS...HEARD...SAW...WHERE YOUR BODY FELT HEAT...OR COLD. THIS WILL LEAD YOU TO THE TRUE FEELING.

TONGUE-TIED
Boy: Ages 8 – 12

Whenever I see Marion…I always get nervous. I stutter…and can't say what I want to say. I really like her…and I know she likes me…but I didn't know how to tell her. Why don't I call her? I thought of it, but then I'd remember who was on the other end…and it'd be…duh…till I hung up. Well, I finally decided what to do…I wrote her a love letter…but I don't know when I'll mail it. No, I'm not chicken…I'm afraid she'll see my name on the envelope and send it back. Have you ever heard of John Alden? He spoke for Miles Standish, who couldn't talk to a girl he liked…like me. Tom…would you mind?

Acting tip:

TENSION IS A MENTAL CRIPPLER AND CAN AFFECT ALL THE WORK YOU'VE DONE ON YOUR ACTING PREPARATION.

UNVEILED
Boy: Ages 8 – 12

Do you know what I heard? I couldn't believe it! When the word gets around, nothing'll be the same again. It's like finding out that what you knew…wasn't true. All right…I'll tell you. Who's the biggest bully in school? Right, Spike Morgan! The terror of Public School 23. Well, he won't be anymore. No, he isn't moving…and for the first time I'm not afraid of him. What happened? Last night I took a short cut and passed his house. Yeah, I know it was dangerous…but I was late for supper…and nothing happened…except I heard and saw him…through the window of his room…wearing glasses and playing the violin!

Acting tip:

IF YOU WANT AN EMOTION TO COME ON STAGE…WORK AGAINST IT…DON'T CRY…DON'T GET EMOTIONAL…BUT CONCENTRATE ON YOUR SENSES…AND IT WILL COME FULLY AND TRUTHFULLY. THINK OF SOAP IN A TUB…THE MORE YOU REACH FOR IT THE FURTHER AWAY IT GETS.

ENTREPENEUR
Boy: Ages 8 – 12

I know what the kids call me. Nut job…jerk…paper pusher! But I don't care. Why? Because I don't want anyone to know it doesn't bother me. I know you're my friend…but it's secret. Top secret! I'd like to tell you…but I can't. You really want to know…don't you? All right…but you've got to swear on all your baseball card collection you'll never tell. Okay, I hope I won't regret this. Dad drives me and my papers to the railroad station early in the morning. He goes to work and I sell my papers to the commuters at the gate. It's a gold mine! Especially when the train's coming in and they can't wait for their change. Once a guy gave me a five dollar bill and told me to keep the change. So, whenever the kids bug me…I'm safe…because they don't know what I know.

Acting tip:

WHEN TRYING TO CAPTURE A SENSORY SENSATION, BE SPECIFIC FOR INSTANCE, DON'T SAY, "I FEEL COLD." INSTEAD TRY TO RECALL SPECIFICALLY WHERE YOU FEEL THE COLD.

TALL TALK
Boy: Ages 8 – 12

Everyone tells me what I'm going to be when I grow up. Grandma wants me to be a doctor...grandpa says I should be a lawyer. Mom thinks I'm going to be a teacher...and daddy? A salesman like him. Well, they're all wrong because I'm not going to be a doctor...or a lawyer...a teacher or a salesman. I think everyone should be what they want to be. Being happy is more important than pleasing everybody else. Sure, I know what I'm going to be when I grow up. My mind's made up...I'm going to be...another Mickey Mantle!

Acting tip:

WHEN CHOOSING AN ACTING TEACHER...ASK TO AUDIT THE CLASS AND DECIDE IF HE OR SHE IS RIGHT FOR YOU. DON'T BE INFLUENCED BY NAMES OF FAMOUS STUDENTS WHO WERE TAUGHT BY THE TEACHER. NOT ALL ACTING TEACHERS ARE RIGHT FOR EVERY STUDENT.

SAFETY FIRST!
Boy: Ages 8 – 12

Nancy, I'm going to be an astronaut! I'll land on the moon…and visit Mars…maybe even Jupiter. What are you laughing for? My mind is made up. I'm serious! I'm reading a lot of books about astronauts. I'm gonna write NASA and ask for an application. I know by the time I'm old enough…I'll be sitting in a spacecraft and waiting! Six…five…four…three…two…one…blast off! I'll wave to you when we're in orbit! Maybe even leave your name on one of the planets. You'll see. What? Do I want to go tree climbing with you? Are you kidding? That's dangerous!

Acting tip:

IN LEARNING LINES REMEMBER THAT IN LIFE WE DON'T PLAN HOW WE ARE GOING TO SPEAK. WE RESPOND WITH OUR FEELINGS AND SITUATIONS.

DOW 'JIMMY' JONES
Boy: Ages 8 – 12

I got a dollar for carrying Mrs. Kissell's groceries. I was passing the A & P when she said, "Jimmy, I'll give you a dollar if you'd carry my groceries." *(Shows dollar.)* I didn't know it was so easy to make money. Who knows, I may start a carry your bag service. What am I going to do with the dollar? Daddy's a stockbroker…so he'll buy computer game stocks. I'll get all my friends to buy the games…daddy'll re-invest all the profits…then I'll be rich before I'm in the sixth grade. Oh, there comes the ice cream truck… *(Looks at dollar.)* y' know, where's my rush? I'm gonna buy a vanilla cone…so I'll just wait till seventh grade before I get rich.

Acting tip:

DO YOUR BEST AND FORGET THE REST.

HAPPINESS IS…
Boy: Ages 9 – 12

Y'know what I do when there's no one around? When everyone's too busy to play…or have to do chores? I go to the movies. Well, I don't really go to the movies. I stand in line with people waiting to see the most popular movie playing. You'll be surprised at how many nice people you can meet and talk to…about all kinds of things. Once they all go in…I wait around and join another line. It sure helps when you're lonely. Y'know sometimes they want to pay for me to see the movie…but I never go…because it's so much more fun outside. Besides, how can you talk to anyone when the movie's on?

Acting tip:

NEVER REPEAT A PREVIOUS PERFORMANCE…ALWAYS DO IT FOR THE FIRST TIME. RECALL THE STEPS YOU TOOK WHICH LED TO THE FEELING OF ACCOMPLISHMENT YOU HAD ACHIEVED.

GREAT NEWS!
Boy: Ages 9 – 13

I think Marion Myers really likes me. I mean she sits in front of me in my third grade class…and I always try to get her to talk to me…but she keeps looking away or hanging around with other boys…but never with me. Once I found out she always goes to the Saturday matinee movie…so I waited till I saw her…then got in line behind her. But she didn't even say, hello! So, why do I think she likes me now? Today in class she turned in her seat, smiled at me, for the first time, and called me an amoeba! I can't wait to look at a dictionary and find out how much she likes me.

Acting tip:

WHILE WAITING YOUR TURN AT AN AUDITION…STUDY YOUR SCRIPT AND AVOID ANYTHING OR ANYONE THAT WILL AFFECT YOUR FOCUS.

DESPERATE!
Boy: Ages 14 – 19

You know what I decided to major in? Art! Yeah, Art! I always wanted to be a painter. Especially after I visited the Museum of Art! Sure, I know it won't be easy to make a living…but right now my main concern is my social life. After that's taken care of I'll think about my future. What am I talking about? I'll tell you. Whenever I go to the museum I see artists with their pallets copying the masters…and they're always surrounded by women. Some are really gorgeous! Well, I figure I'll bring my palette and paint, and wait till she comes. At least I'll know right off the bat that we have something in common. So, I figure with a couple of strokes from my paint brush…I'll find her!

Acting tip:

FIND SIMILARITIES WITHIN YOURSELF THAT CORRESPONDS TO THE CHARACTER YOU'RE PLAYING.

TWO OF A KIND!
Boy: Ages 13 – 17

Do you know what's wrong with me? No, don't tell me...I'll tell you! I'm shy. You're wrong...I really am, and I'm not proud of it... why should I be? Maybe it's my upbringing or even genes...all I really know is how I feel. No matter what I do...it doesn't help. What do you mean things'll change when I get older! I'm not interested in what happens then...it's now that's important. I like Amy...I really do. We meet on the school bus everyday and all we say is..."Hi!" She sits next to me in economics...and I want to write a note to her about taking her to the movies...or for a pizza. But I can't, even though I'm always catching her giving me the eye. But y' know what I really like about her? We have something in common. She's shy, too! So, maybe there's still some hope. You're right...I'm going to take your advice...thanks. So what am I worrying about? This afternoon on the bus...I'm going to give her a wink...before she eyes me...that's it! I'm going to break the ice...and sit not in back or front but next to her. Fred, I'm so glad we talked...it really helped having a buddy like you. Wanna be my best man?

Acting tip:

THE ACTOR MUST NOT ONLY SPEAK WORDS BUT ALLOW THOUGHTS TO MAKE THE WORDS BELIEVABLE.

THE NAME GAME!
Boy: Ages 10 – 15

Did y' ever wonder about how places got their names? I mean like...Gary, Indiana...then there's Glen's Falls...Phil...adelphia...Ken ...tucky...Charlotte...Fay...etville...Elizabeth...and how about Bill... ings? They must have been named after people who did something with their lives and are remembered for it. If when I grow up and invent something...or become a famous astronaut...or even President...they'll never name anything after me... and it's not fair...unless I change my name. What do I mean? When did they ever name a place after a cat? Especially Felix?

Acting tip:

WHATEVER YOU ARE PHYSICALLY USE IT ON A STAGE. DON'T HIDE, DENY OR PRETEND IT DOESN'T EXIST... ACCEPT IT AS PART OF THE CHARACTER. USE IT!

SURPRISE!
Boy: Ages 10 – 15

It's been a year since my grandpa died...I wish he was still here. I'm sorry you never met him...he was the best grandpa ever. Whenever he visited us...he always wore a coat. My favorite was his winter one, because it had the deepest pockets and was always filled with candy...and all kinds of presents like baseball cards...new pens and cassette tapes. I miss going through them. We have the overcoat in the closet. When I get married and have children...I'm going to tell my dad to wear the coat so they'll get surprises like I did.

Acting tip:

STAGE RELAXATION IS THAT BALANCE BETWEEN FULL ENERGY AND THE FEELING OF EASE. STAGE ENERGY IS HIGHER THAN LIFE ENERGY WHEN COUPLED WITH PHYSI-CAL RELAXATION IS THE STATE YOU SHOULD BE IN WHEN PERFORMING.

DO OR DIE!
Boy: Ages 16 – 20

Some people think life isn't fair. They think others have all the luck. I guess that's human nature…but I think it's a load of bull! Look at Christopher Reeve…he had everything going for him…until he had his accident. But he didn't throw in the towel…because he knew that once he did…life would be over…before it was. I'm not Superman…but I know what I'm talking about. Fred…you know me…I've been physically challenged from birth…and like Christopher Reeve, I'll never and will never let it stop me from living my life to the fullest. I know people stare at the way I walk…but I don't allow it to bother me…why should I? Well, Fred, I've got to go now…because I've got a lifetime of things to do!

Acting tip:

LEARN HOW TO DO…NOT WHAT TO DO!

THE WAY IT WAS!
Boy: Ages 12 – 16

The world isn't what it used to be, George. My grandpa tells me about when he was young and there was no television. No computers...and no Nintendo. He said he listened to radio...yeah, you heard me...radio! He used a typewriter...and spent most of his time playing all kind of games with his friends. During summer vacation...they'd all stay up late...and talk...or hang around the candy store...walk around the neighborhood...meet girls under street lamps...kid around and go home. No one was shooting guns...or shooting up...just shooting the breeze. Hey, movies used to cost a quarter...for two movies! Now movies cost an arm and a leg...and we spend most of our lives watching the tube. The streets aren't safe anymore...so what else can we do? Y' know...I really wish I lived in grandpa's day. Uh, huh, I thought you'd feel the same.

Acting tip:

FIND YOUR INNER LIFE.

GENES

Boy: Ages 12 – 16

I'm such a clod! I admit it! Whenever something has to be done…I always mess up. Like when I leave my homework at home, and the teacher gives me a 'D'. Mom told me to open a can of tuna fish the other day…and I opened cat food! Yeah, I did! I even forget everybody's birthday. I guess I'll never change. How can I? Almost everyday at home I hear a dish break…dad's always locking his keys in the car…or forgets where he puts his glasses. Sis always forgets to brush her teeth…and loses her pens. So, I can't help goofing up. Yeah, you're right…no one's perfect…but who am I kidding? There's nothing I can do about it…it runs in the family!

Acting tip:

DO A RELAXATION EXERCISE IN YOUR DRESSING ROOM AT HALF-HOUR BEFORE CURTAIN.

WHAT'S IN A NAME?
Boy: Ages 13 – 16

I don't know why my parents named me George? Why not Mark...or Larry...or even Michael like yours? No, it had to be George! I can't stand it! Everybody either laughs or looks at me funny. And then come the jokes...or comparisons! What's worse, I'm stuck with it for life! I mean if I meet a girl I really liked and wanted to marry...and especially if her name was Martha...would she...after she found out her second name would be Washington?

Acting tip:

IMPROVISATIONS ARE USED TO HELP ACTORS EXPLORE AND INCREASE THEIR UNDERSTANDING OF THEIR CHAR-ACTERS WITHIN A SCENE.

HIP HEAP
Boy: Ages 16 – 20

Well, it happened again, George. Yeah, I had another personal ad blind date…and it ended like all the rest. A zero! Oh, we got along great! She had a dynamite figure and a face to match. We even had a lot in common…and set a date for the weekend. Can you guess what happened? Right! The test! We went out to the parking lot and I introduced her to my 'Smithsonian Special!' And you know she was like all the rest. "That's your car? How old is it? Does it run?" I told her it survived six presidents. She almost fainted! Maybe they all ought to stop answering or putting in personal ads…and stake out car showrooms. I know I'll never hear from her again. That heap of mine'll keep me single till I trade it in for brand new wheels.

Acting tip:

CHOOSE PHRASES AND IMAGES THAT WILL STIR UP AN EMOTIONAL RESPONSE: BE SPECIFIC.

HEART TO HEART!
Boy: Ages 15 – 19

Dad, I've got to talk to you. Put your paper down and listen…it's important! No…it can't wait! I should have told you a long time ago…but I kept putting it off. I don't know why…maybe I didn't want to hurt you…or was afraid you'd hate me. But it isn't fair to either of us. You wanted me to be a man. You told me not to cry…fight my own battles…even lift weights…but you never really know who or what I was. *(Puts hand up.)* No, dad, let me finish. You always taught me not to be afraid, well, I'm taking your advice and I'm grateful to you for giving me the courage to finally tell you. Dad, I'm gay…have been for years. Why are you looking at me like that? Like what? Like…I committed a crime! Who's the brave one now?

Acting tip:

AFFECTIVE MEMORY OR EMOTIONAL RECALL IS A TOOL USED TO RECAPTURE A FEELING YOU HAD EXPERIENCED IN YOUR PAST. IT SHOULD NOT BE DONE IF YOU ARE STILL INVOLVED IN A SEVERE EMOTIONAL DISTURBANCE. AT FIRST THE EXERCISE SHOULD BE SUPERVISED BY A COMPETENT TEACHER.

DECIBLES!
Boy: Ages 15 – 19

Die Hard one two and three…and the rest of those high voltage…car crashing…gun crazy pictures…all turn me off. Sure, I know they're box office hits, but what about a guy who's trying to get close to a chick? You've got your arms around her, lean over…pucker up…and vroom…the theater shakes like there was an explosion! It's a downer! You know what I mean? The moment's shot to hell! But I figured it out. If I'm trying to get close to a date…romantically…I take her to a little art movie house in town…that only plays silent films!

Acting tip:

WHEN PERFORMING A MONOLOGUE HAVE A SPECIFIC PERSON IN MIND AND WITH YOUR SENSES LOOK AT THAT PERSON AS IF HE OR SHE WERE THERE. TRY TO SEE THE PERSON'S FACE…THE NOSE…EYES…HAIR…SMILE…THE BODY. IT'S NOT THAT YOU SEE THAT IMAGINARY PERSON BUT THAT YOU ARE TRYING TO SEE HIM OR HER.

FILLING THE VOID!
Boy: Ages 15 – 18

Rufus and I are the best of friends. He's always around when I need him. He gives me his paw, wags his tail whenever I come home, and barks when I ask him to. He never wants much from me…just to be fed, petted, walked and loved. What more can anyone ask for? He's a great dog. Sure, he's only a mutt…and other dog owners keep their pedigrees away from him…and he's too small to stand up against bigger dogs…and is always shedding…but, so what? I'm not perfect, either. I don't date because I'm not popular. I can't make the school teams…I'm never elected to any offices…and my parent's aren't rich. But it doesn't matter to Rufus. I wish more people could be like him. *(Calls)* RUFUS! Here, boy!

Acting tip:

TO COUNTER THE NEED TO HOLD ON TO THE WORDS…TRY THE EXERCISE OF TALKING GIBBERISH WHILE REHEARSING TO FIND YOUR INNER LINE.

GRAFFITI
Boy: Ages 14 – 17

Don't you hate graffiti? It's all over the place! Paul, wherever you go, there are ugly spray painted signs on walls, sidewalks, I even saw one on a police car. It said PSI! Whatever the heck that means? What's the matter with kids? If they want to be remembered, then why don't they do something like becoming a famous ballplayer, or go to the moon, or invent a better computer? I mean graffiti's not only ugly, but it shows how little the jerks think of themselves. You know what I mean. Hey, let me borrow your penknife…I wanna put a heart with Barbara's 'n my name on this tree trunk. Naw, it's not graffiti…it's love!

Acting tip:

WHEN DOING A SCENE FROM A PLAY IN CLASS, BE CAREFUL THAT YOU REVEAL ONLY WHAT IS CALLED FOR IN THAT PARTICULAR SCENE. UNDERSTAND THE ENTIRE PLAY BUT CONCENTRATE ON PLAYING ONLY THAT PART OF THE PIECE YOU ARE INVOLVED IN AT THE TIME.

OOPS!

Boy: Ages 14 – 18

I finally had a date with Gloria. We went ice skating yesterday. It was great! Some guys think that by doing figure eights...or spins...or leaps...that their dates'll be won over. Well, they're all wrong. The way I figure it, if you really want to get close to a girl like Gloria you've gotta go the other way. What did I do? I kept Gloria, you've falling down all over the rink. Yeah, I know I'm a fair skater...but Gloria didn't know. She kept trying to keep me from hitting the ice so many times, you'd think we were both joined with crazy glue. I can still feel her arms all over me. She never let go. It was fantastic! And she wants to go again! Take it from me, Arthur...if you wanna really get close to a chick...get thee to a skating rink and break the ice.

Acting tip:

LEARN YOUR LINES: PARAPHRASING THE LINES IN A PERFORMANCE WILL NOT ONLY NEGATIVBELY AFFECT THE PLAY BUT ALSO WHAT YOU ARE TRYING TO ACHIEVE IN THE ROLE.

LOOK BEFORE YOU LEAP!
Boy: Ages Late Teens

Y' wanna know how I tell what a broad'll look when she gets older? I make sure I get a good look at her mother. Look, it's like investing in your future. I mean you wouldn't sink dough in a stock or bank that was a bummer, right? You'd check 'em out. Well, that goes for getting serious with a chick. Who wants t' wake up screamin'? I read all the time about how long term marriages break up because the guy digs a younger dame. Well, as far as I'm concerned it was the old man's mistake because he didn't do his homework before he got hitched.

Acting tip:

WHEN A DIRECTOR AT AN AUDITION ASKS YOU TO PLAY A SCENE ANOTHER WAY HE USUALLY WANTS TO SEE HOW YOU TAKE DIRECTION.

JUST MY LUCK!
Boy: Ages Late Teens

That's it! What's the use? Who cares? I've had it! Look, if it weren't meant to be it would have been by now. I guess nothing is sure in this world but death and taxes. But I'm too young to die…and don't make enough to pay taxes. So, why is it always happening to me? Y' know it's like you find something you think is valuable…and it turns out to be a zero. What am I bitching about? Remember, Helen? The one I introduced you to last week? Yeah, she was a looker. Was? You bet was! Her parents are moving to the end of the world! Where? Portland, Oregon! I thought we might have a future…now all we'll have is Email or our cell phones. I swear it never fails. And it all started when I was born. I just wish my mother didn't give birth to me on a Friday the Thirteenth!

Acting tip:

DON'T BECOME A CLASSROOM ACTOR: APPLY WHAT YOU'VE LEARNED BY PERFORMING BEFORE AN AUDIENCE.

FALSE IDENTITY
Boy: Ages 15 – 19

I never believed that life would be easy. When I was in my teens, I found out it isn't...and it hasn't improved. Look at me! What do you see? I'm a normal guy. I like to play tennis...go to the movies...and on occasion I even eat junk food. So, what's bugging me? Well, I'll tell you. When I was in high school, some guys started spreading the rumor I was gay. Do you know how it feels to be laughed at? Shoved? Read blackboards with the words, 'Arthur Kelly's king of the fags?' Now here I am...trying to make it...but the stigma and memories still follow me. I know I'm not alone...but what makes it so difficult is that I'm not gay! Never have been! Yet, I still feel the stares and pain. What should I do? Carry a sign around my neck, 'I'M NOT GAY?' There's one thing I've learned is that everyone has the right to be who and what they are. I'm not gay...but even if I were...I'd never let anyone make me feel less about myself. Because once you do, then life wouldn't be worth living.

Acting tip:

THEATER TRADE PAPERS LIKE BACKSTAGE, SHOW BUSINESS AND ROSS REPORTS GIVE YOU ACCESS TO CASTING CALLS AND CONTACTS FOR AGENTS AND CASTING DIRECTORS.

COVERING THE BASES
Boy: Ages 16 – 19

Who am I? Well, it's summer ain't it? So, it's Gracie! Sheila? Aw I won't be seeing her till winter. Barbara's spring. Autumn's Angel. What's the big deal and what am I getting at? Well, I'll tell you! It's just a case of putting things in their time and place. Gracie'n I love the beach…Sheila's a skiing freak…like me. When the leaves change…it's Angel! Barb's my blooming budding buddy. Sure, I know that one day I'll have to settle down with one skirt…but till I do…I'll just have to be a man for all seasons! Got it?

Acting tip:

DIFFERENT ACTORS ARE TENSE IN DIFFERENT PARTS OF THEIR BODIES. IT IS IMPORTANT THAT YOU RECOGNIZE WHERE YOUR TENSIONS ARE SO YOU CAN DEAL WITH THEM.

BECKWOURTH
Boy: (Black) Ages 14 – 17

Who am I, pa? You say I'm your son but others say I belong to you. I'm confused. Been that way since I c'n remember. 'N it pains me. They never let up...so I figure since they won' accept me as an equal, than I've got to make my own way...in any way I see fit. Pa, m' insides cry-out whenever I think of goin' west...or hear tales the trappers tell. You crossed the Mississippi many times 'n come back...well I won' be worth nothin' till I go, too. Pa, I'm goin' west no matter what y' say, 'n one day hen I come back, I'll be rich 'n famous, 'n looked up to...by everyone. I'll walk the streets of Saint Lou...and people'll move aside 'n I'll hear 'em sayin'...."There goes Jim Beckwourth...ain' he some-thin'?"

Acting tip:

ACTING IS NOT FUN...IT'S HARD WORK.

SURPRISE!
Boy: Ages 16 – 19

I swear that's the last time I answer a personal ad! I don't mind that they exaggerate everything about themselves. I mean, if Ford wanted to sell their cars they wouldn't admit they give poor gas mileage…or have poor brakes…or have no styling. No one would buy a Ford…or answer a personal ad! So, what's a guy to do when an ad says she's vivacious…knock out gorgeous…and has fantastic legs? You call! We spoke on the phone and I couldn't wait to meet her. We met last night and she was the exact opposite of how she described herself. Now I know that beauty's only skin deep… but did she have to have so much skin?

Acting tip:

WHEN CHOOSING AN ACTING TEACHER TRY TO AUDIT THE CLASS OR CHECK OUT BOOKS LISTING QUALIFIED ACTING COACHES. ASK OTHER ACTORS FOR THEIR RECOMMENDATIONS AND CHOOSE A TEACHER YOU ARE COMPATIBLE WITH.

LOST LOVE
Boy: Ages 16 – 19

The phone rang this morning...and I knew it was Ellen. That's when she always phoned. It started my day off with a bang. But this time she didn't sound right...I mean...for two years there always was a sparkle and laugh in her voice...but they were missing. She told me not to call her again...because she was in love with someone else. I don't know who...I don't want to know. It painful! It's the first time something like this ever happened to me. I mean, I'm only seventeen...and I don't think I'll ever trust another woman again! *(Close to tears.)* It hurts too much.

Acting tip:

SAY A LINE WHILE HEARING AN IMAGINARY AND SPECIFIC SAD TUNE. THEN LISTEN TO AN IMAGINARY UP TUNE. NOTICE HOW THE WORDS TAKE ON A DIFFERENT MEANING AND RHYTHM.

ULTERIOR MOTIVE!
Boy: Ages 16 – 19

Everybody's all beat out of shape because I don't own a car. Dad said he's gonna buy a new Accord...and offered me his Buick...yeah...his Le Sabre. It's only three years old...but I don't want it! Mom and my sister Carol think I'm nuts...well that's their problem. I like the way things are. Why? Hey, if I got a date...and I use my dad's wheels nothing'll be the same. What's the deal? All right, I'll clue you in! Why do you think I'm always dating the classiest chicks? I'll give you a clue. How do you think I get to school? Right! I hitchhike! It gives me a chance to meet the best lookers in town. I just wait on the road...watch out for the doll I like behind the wheel...but never put my thumb out till they pass muster...then it's a match! *(Laughs)* Own a car...and there goes my social life.

Acting tip:

I CAN EXPLAIN HOW YOUR SENSES WILL REACT TO AN IMAGINARY OBJECT. YOU CAN MAKE YOUR SENSES BELIEVE ANYTHING AS THOUGH IT ACTUALLY EXISTED. THINK OF LOOKING AT AN OVERSIZED, SLICED JUICY LEMON...SEE WHAT I MEAN?

WRONG AGAIN!
Boy: Ages 16 – 19

I met the baddest looking chick at the mall yesterday. She winked at me and I got her message and moved in. "Hi!" I said. "How are you? I guess it must be my lucky day…I mean to get a wink from a looker like you on the mall's too good to be true." And she was alone…like me. I have to admit I had my eyes on her when we both were at the Gap. She had a great figure…and I kept thinking how super she'd look in tight jeans. I told her, "I go to the beach a lot…are you into bikinis?" She didn't say anything so I finally introduced myself…and she shot me down! Yeah, she did! She said, "Sorry, Jack…you got the wrong message. I didn't wink at you…I had something in my eye!"

Acting tip:

THE JAZZING UP EXERCISE: MARCH ENERGETICALLY IN A CIRCLE OR IN PLACE THEN START A TUNE…BUT HOLD ON AND ELONGATE EACH SYLLABLE…THEN CHANGE THE RHYTHMS AND CONTINUE SINGING THE TUNE…WITH EACH RHYTHM CHANGE…THE SOUNDS SHOULD FOLLOW THE BODIES MOVEMENTS: IT IS AN EXERCISE TO HELP YOU BREAK AWAY FROM HOLDING ON TO THE WORDS AND ALLOW THE MOVEMENTS TO COLOR THE WORDS.

MONOLOGUES
for
BOYS or GIRLS

GROWING UP!
Boy/Girl: Ages 5 – 9

Mommy, what happens to children when they grow up? I mean what games do they play...and how early do they have to go to bed? Do they still have the same friends...and what do they watch on television? Why? I just want to know. Yeah, I know everybody has to grow up...but I don't know if I want to...huh? It's because after I grow up...then I'll never see Big Bird again!

Acting tip:

ACTING IS LIKE LIVING UNDER IMAGINARY CIRCUM-STANCES. ACTING IS NOT MAKING BELIEVE...ACTING IS BELIEVING.

MOTHERHOOD
Boy/Girl: Ages 6 – 10

My cat Misty is going to be a mother. No, she didn't tell me, silly. But I know. It was easy. When mom gave birth to my little brother, Jimmy, dad always had to get her all kinds of different things…like pickles. She used to hate pickles. She got vanilla ice cream…instead of chocolate…and even Hydrox instead of Oreos. Well, that's how I found out about Misty. This whole week she won't eat anything she used to like…and ate what she never ate before. You want a kitten?

Acting tip:

INVOLUNTARY PHYSICAL MOVEMENTS ON A STAGE TENDS TO DISSIPATE EMOTIONS. IT IS LIKE LETTING AIR OUT OF A BALLOON. THE BANG WHEN PUNCTURED IS DIMINISHED.

CAREERS
Boy/Girl: Ages 6 – 10

(Carrying books.) Hi, Frank…no, I can't play today. Can't go to the movies, either. I've gotta go home. I have to take care of Spot. He's sick…so I went to the library alnd took out these books about helping sick dogs. I'm going to make him feel better. Who knows…when I grow up…I may go to college and become a vegetarian!

Acting tip:

STRIVE TO BRING TO THE STAGE WHAT EVERY HUMAN BEING DOES NATURALLY IN LIFE.

GO FOR IT!
Boy/Girl: Ages 7 – 10

No one believes I taught Fluffy to beg…and give me her paw…and even to roll over. They kept telling me cats don't do dog tricks…well, they were wrong! You know I feel like Christopher Columbus…go ahead and laugh…they all laughed at him, too! They made fun of him and kept telling him the world was flat…and that he'd fall off the earth. But he tried…and you know what happened. Yeah, I taught Fluffy, but she taught me something, too…that anything can happen if you don't listen to negative people and just try. *(Smiles)* Well, I've gotta go…gonna teach Fluffy some more tricks!

Acting tip:

ACTORS MUST DEVOTE THEIR WHOLE LIVES TO LEARNING THEIR CRAFT. THERE IS NO BEGINNING AND NO END TO LEARNING.

AGING!
Boy/Girl: Ages 7 – 10

Harold, how old do you think Mrs. Gibney is? Some kids say she's been the school librarian since it opened. She always wears old lady dresses…and glasses…and keeps forgetting where she puts things…and she's always typing on a typewriter instead of a computer. Yes, a typewriter! I even see gray in her hair. Yeah, she's old alright…I'll bet she must be forty!

Acting tip:

IT'S NOT THE SIZE OF THE ROLE BUT THE ACTOR WHO PER-FORMS IT AS TRUTHFULLY AND WITH THE SAME ENTUSI-ASM AS HE OR SHE WOULD A LARGER PART.

STAYING AFLOAT!
Boy/Girl: Ages 7 – 10

Guess what! I learned to swim! It happened this morning at the pool. My dad was holding me, then said, "Kick your feet and move your arms!" Well, I did…and then he let me go. I was so scared! I mean I could've drowned…but I didn't. I swam! Isn't that great? It really wasn't so hard. Maybe some day I'll swim the English channel or win a gold medal at the Olympics…and be famous. I only hope they'll let me keep wearing my water-wings.

Acting tip:

NEVER WORK FOR THE RESULT: IT'S LIKE CLIMBING A MOUNTAIN…YOU MUST START FROM THE BOTTOM AND STEP BY STEP REACH THE SUMMIT.

VERNAL EQUINOX
Boy/Girl: Ages 7 – 10

Vernon, do you know what I hate about summer? It has to end! No more swimming…no more getting up late…not having to do homework…and worst of all…no more playing outdoors till the sun goes down. Soon, whenever I get home from school it'll be almost time to get ready for bed. If I had my way, summer would never end! *(Thinks)* But then…they'll be no sledding on the hill…no trick or treating…and I'll never get my new roller blades for Christmas. *(Thinks)* Hmm, maybe it's not all that bad. Well, I better go…gotta get my winter clothes out of the attic! *(Singing)* Jingle Bells!

Acting tip:

IF YOU CONCENTRATE ON FORCING A FEELING THE TRUE EMOTION WILL NOT APPEAR.

TUMMY ACHE
Boy/Girl: Ages 9 – 14

Mom says I've got to watch what I eat. She says fat and cholesterol are unhealthy, so whenever I have my school lunch or even at home…it's no eggs…butter…cookies…hamburgers…ice cream…bacon…and especially no Twinkies. Now all I can eat are salads without dressing…fish…skinless chicken…and fruit. If this keeps up I may grow up to be the healthiest and hungriest adult! *(Pathetic)* You wouldn't have an Oreo would you?

Acting tip:

IF YOU WANT TO KEEP A PLAYWRIGHT HAPPY…DON'T PARAPHRASE! SAY THE WORDS AS THEY ARE WRITTEN.

THE WHITE LIE
Boy/Girl: Ages 8 – 12

Hi, Amy! It's me! Yeah, it all turned out fine and it really wasn't too bad. I know I expected a lecture at least...or worse! That was until I got an idea. When I got home I told mom and dad about how Diane Davis ran away because she lost her school lunch money. I said that the cops came to school and were looking for her. I saw her parents crying..."Diane...Diane...where's our little girl?" And that it went on for hours! The cops said they'll start searching all the lakes and ponds...and woods...and call the F. B. I. Mom was very upset and said she couldn't believe Diane would run away because she lost her lunch money. She said, "Nothing's worth more than having your child." She cried and hugged me...until I told her..."Mom, it wasn't Diane who lost her lunch money....I lost mine!

Acting tip:

EVEN WHEN YOU ARE PORTRAYING A CHARACTER IN AN EMOTIONAL FRENZY...YOU MUST STILL CREATE IN A RELAXED STATE.

ON SECOND THOUGHT!
Boy/Girl: Ages 8 – 12

I'm not going to school tomorrow. I know it's not a holiday…I just don't feel like it. I'm going to get sick. I'll just start coughing and moaning, and tell mommy my throat hurts. Then she'll let me stay home, and I'll sleep late…play *(BOY: Nintendo. GIRL: with my dolls.)*, listen to my CD's. But when she takes my temperature…and I stop coughing…then she'll know I was faking. Then she'll make me do homework…or clean my room…do the dishes…or even mow the lawn. Aw, what's the use…it's not fair! Aw, forget about it….I'll see you on the school bus.

Acting tip:

IF YOU FEEL NERVOUS BEFORE A PERFOMANCE…DON'T TRY TO HIDE IT…REALIZE THAT IT IS YOUR BODY AND MIND TELLING YOU THAT SOMETHING DIFFERENT IS HAPPENING: USE THE NERVOUSNESS BY ALLOWING IT TO ADD TO YOUR CREATI ITY.

TAKE THE MONEY!
Boy/Girl: Ages 10 – 16

My dad's 40 years old. I mean he doesn't look 40. Does he? I mean he always exercises…and beats everyone at tennis. He's still got his own teeth…and jogs three miles a day. Yeah, every day! But he's 40 years old! Soon he'll be 50…then 60…then as old as grandma and grandpa. Y' know sometimes you think everything'll stay the same…but I know it won't. Look, would you mind if we didn't go to the park today? I don't feel like it. I've gotta go…I need to hug my dad!

Acting tip:

USE IMPROVISATIONS SPARINGLY. THEY HELP YOU SAY THE LINES THE WAY YOU WOULD LIKE TO SAY THEM, BUT THEY…WITH OVERUSE, CAN ALTER THE PLAYWRITE'S INTENTIONS.

LETTING GO!
Boy/Girl: Ages 14 – 18

Want a typewriter? It's used and it's old but it still works. I've got extra ribbons…and white out…and paper. No, it's not electric. My dad owned it for years. He gave it to me when I was ten. I remember it was the best present I ever got. Dad was sick then, and wanted me to have it before he died. I hate giving it away, but dad always said nothing should go to waste. Since I got a new computer…well, I won't be needing the typewriter anymore. I suppose you can't hold on to memories forever. All I ask is to treat it gently. It still means a lot to me. And Larry, would you mind if I visited it sometimes and hit a few keys?

Acting tip:

NEVER GO FOR A LAUGH IN A PLAY OR YOU MAY KILL WHAT COULD MAKE IT FUNNY.

FRIENDSHIP
Boy/Girl: Ages 15 – 19

Y' know I can't figure out why I always feel closer to the friends I choose then the family I was born into. Take us for instance…do we argue? Right, sure we don't agree about everything but we always do things together…and talk all the time. Dysfunctional families are the pits! My brothers and Ellen are always too busy…or not interested. Sure, there are other families that aren't too close, but that doesn't make it right. Maybe that's why so many kids run away. No, I'll never do it…because I'd miss you too much.

Acting tip:

AFTER REHEARSALS ARE DONE THE WORK SHOULD DISAP-PEAR: AS YOU PERFORM…SPONTANEITY SHOULD PREVAIL.

TAKING A BREATHER!
Boy/Girl: Ages 7 – 12

I asked my mom why grandpa sleeps so much. Yeah, I know he's old...like all grandpa's...but mom said, "He was a soldier in a big war, and after the war he worked as a mailman and carried a heavy bag for a long time...he even went through the depression." It's when people were very poor...but he still raised five children with grandma till she died. So, I guess that's why he's so tired now. I was going to wake him up...so we can play...but I changed my mind. He needs to sleep. Wanna go swimming?

Acting tip:

INSPIRATION SOMETIMES COMES AND SOMETIMES IT DOES-N'T. DON'T FORCE IT: ALLOW IT TO COME NATURALLY.

Also by
Mark Weston...

Beckwourth

Beckwourth: The Later Years

Winning Monologues from the Beginnings Workshop

Please visit our website **bakersplays.com** for complete descriptions and licensing information.

CPSIA information can be obtained at www.ICGtesting.com
Printed in the USA
LVOW070908290212

270926LV00007B/3/P

9 780874 402629